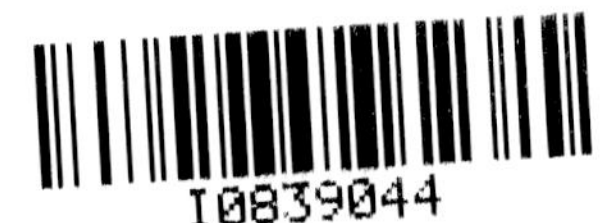

Coloring book for adults and kids amazing panda image for design

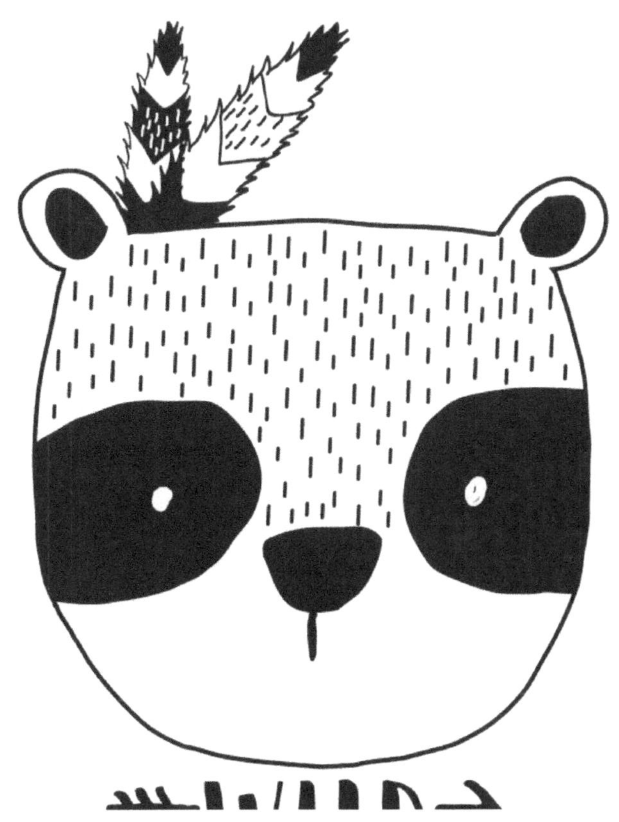

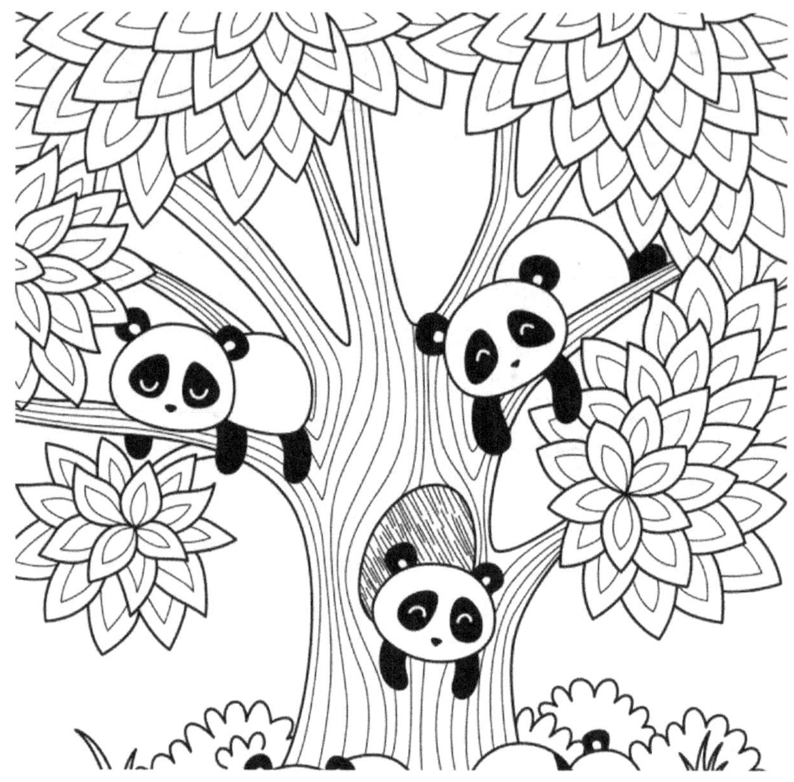

This coloring book is belongs to

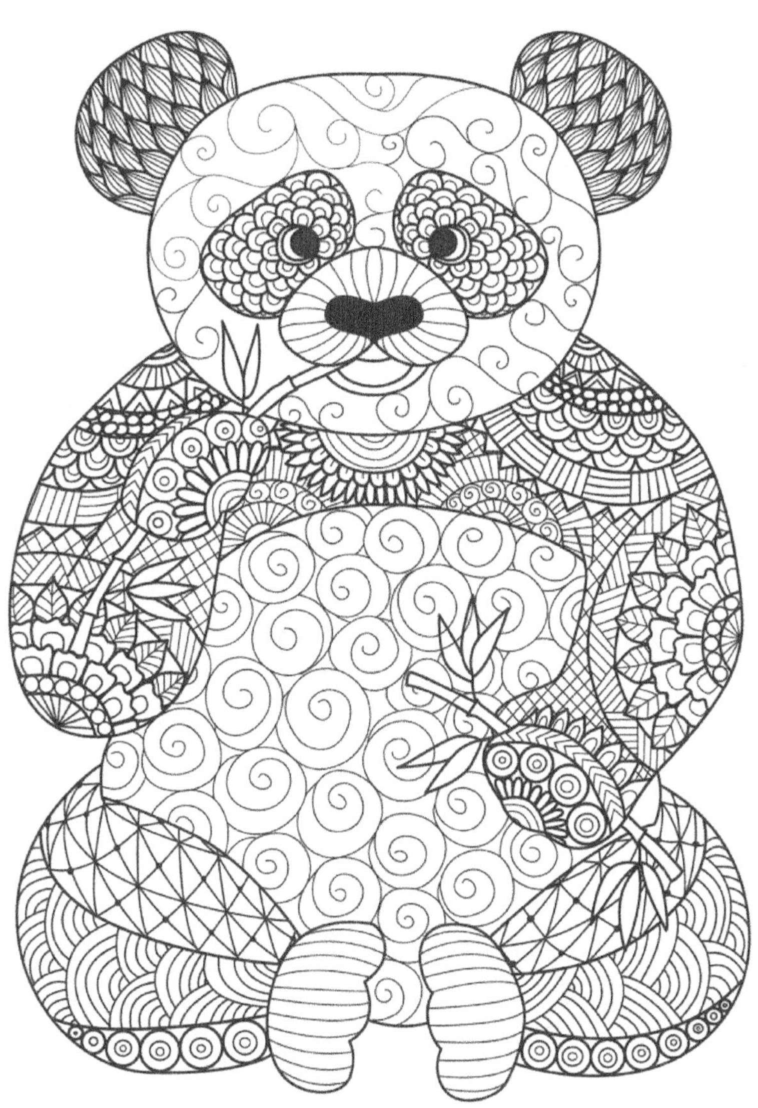

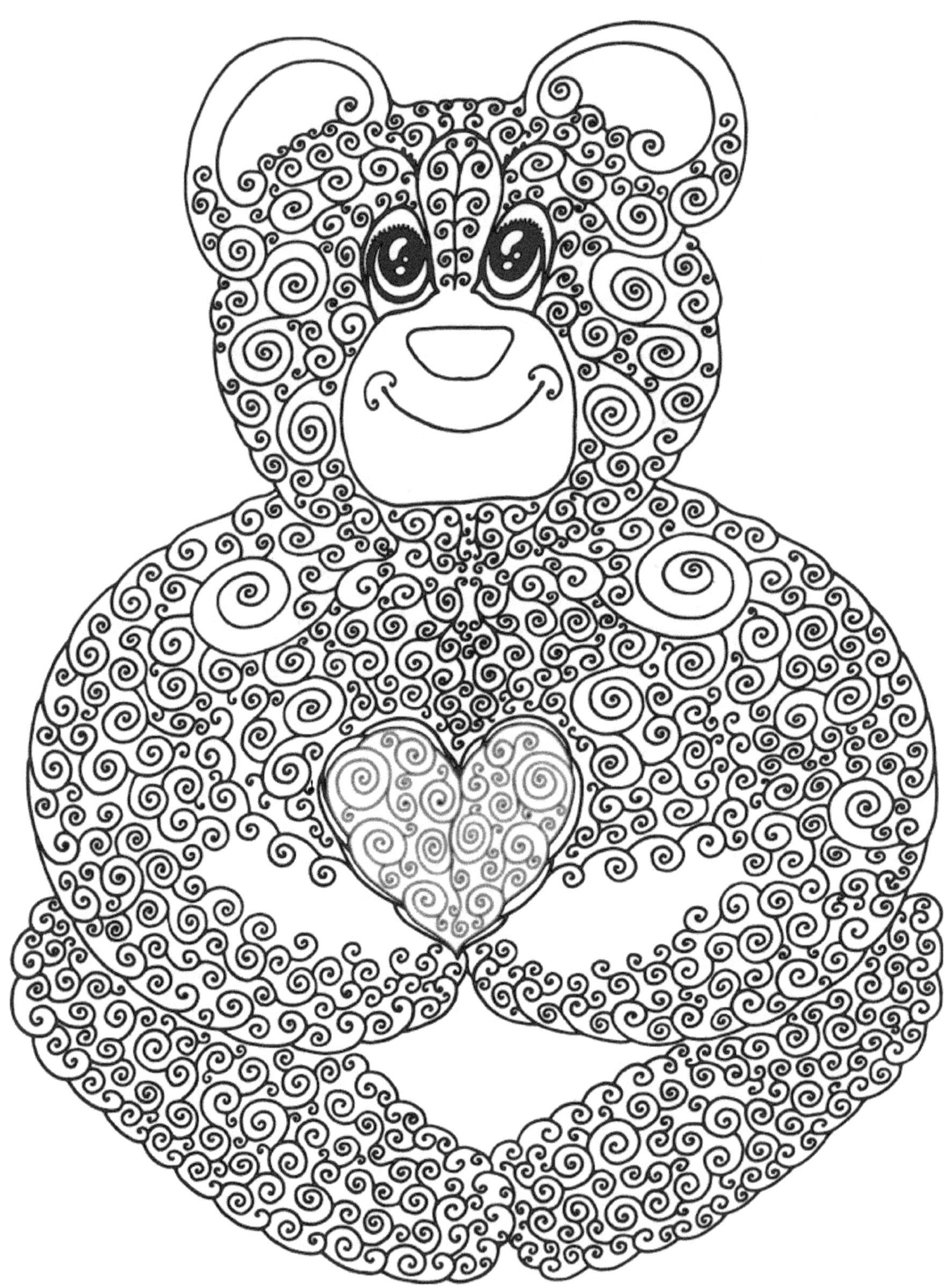

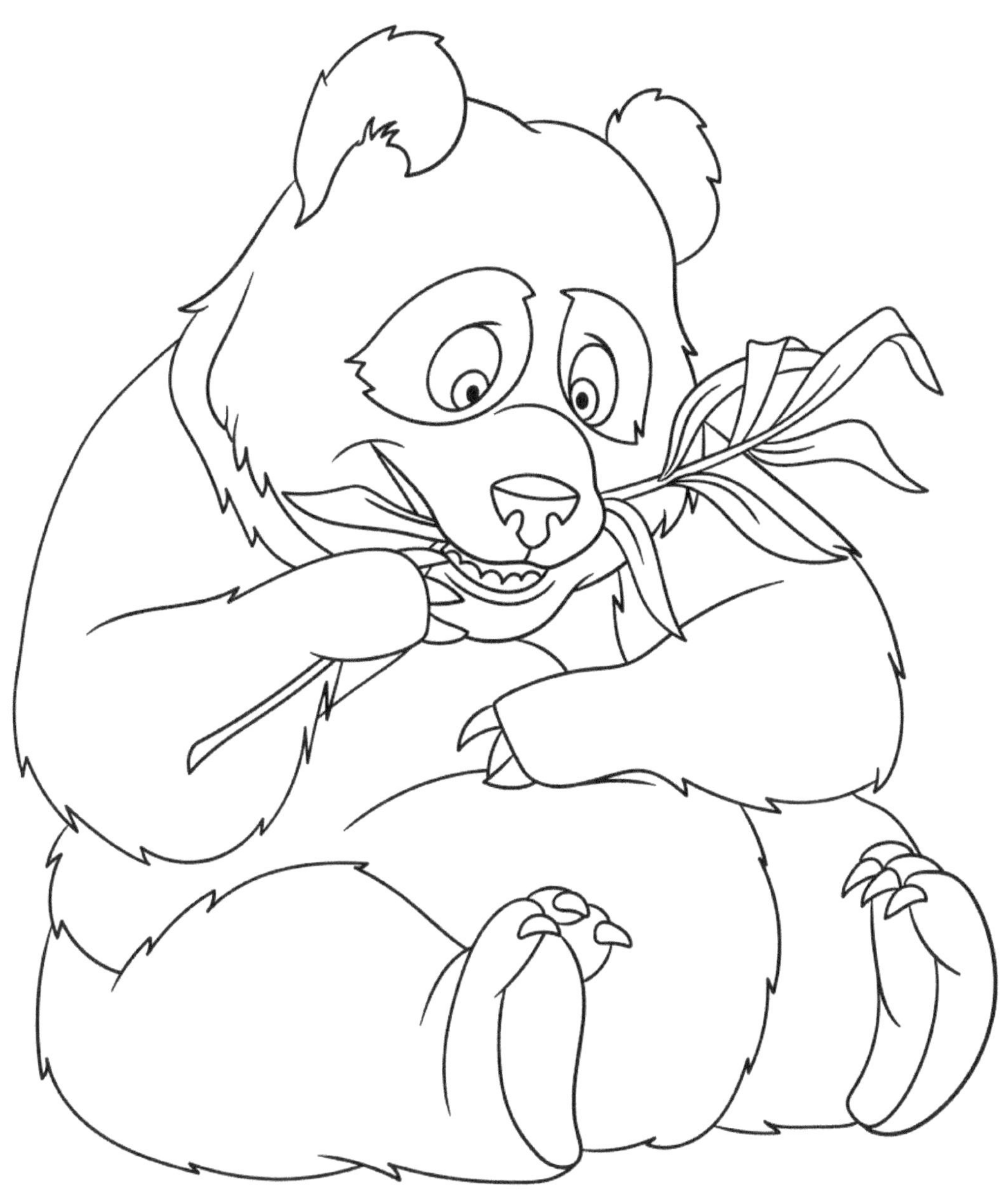

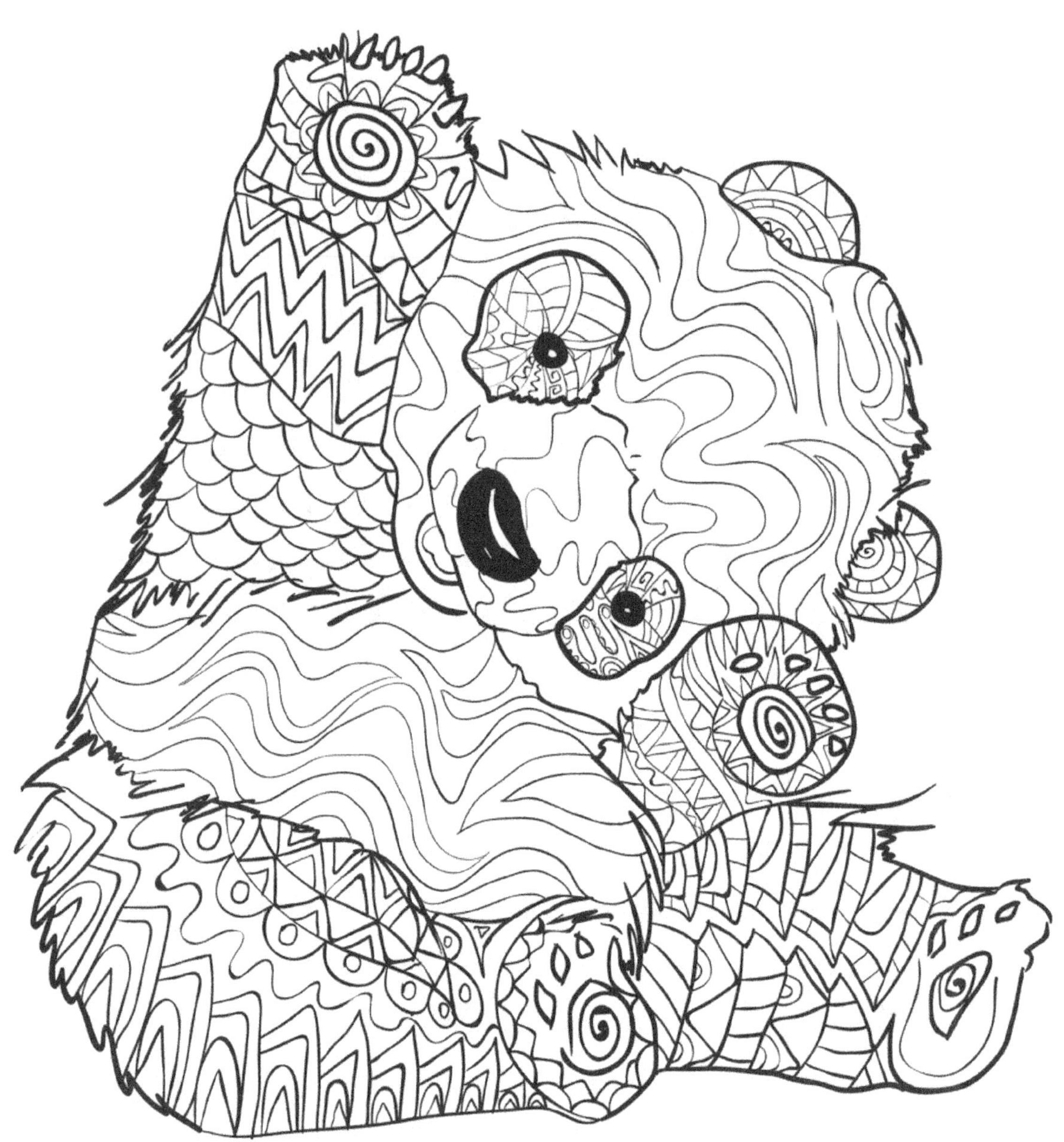

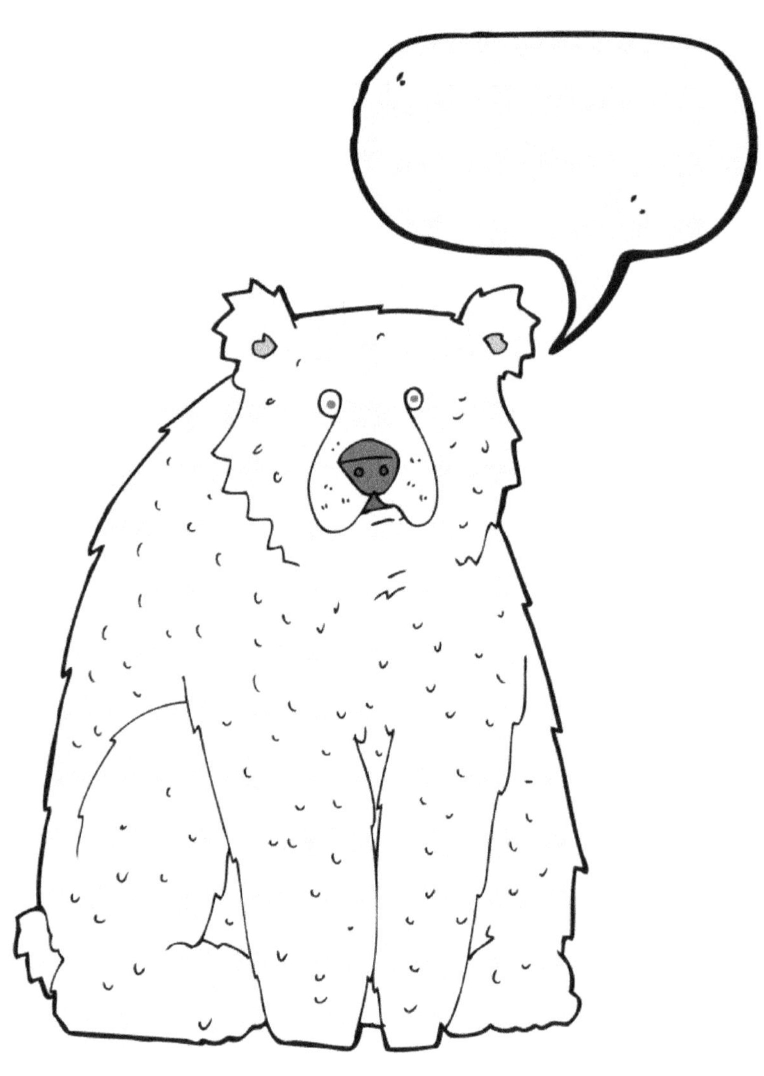

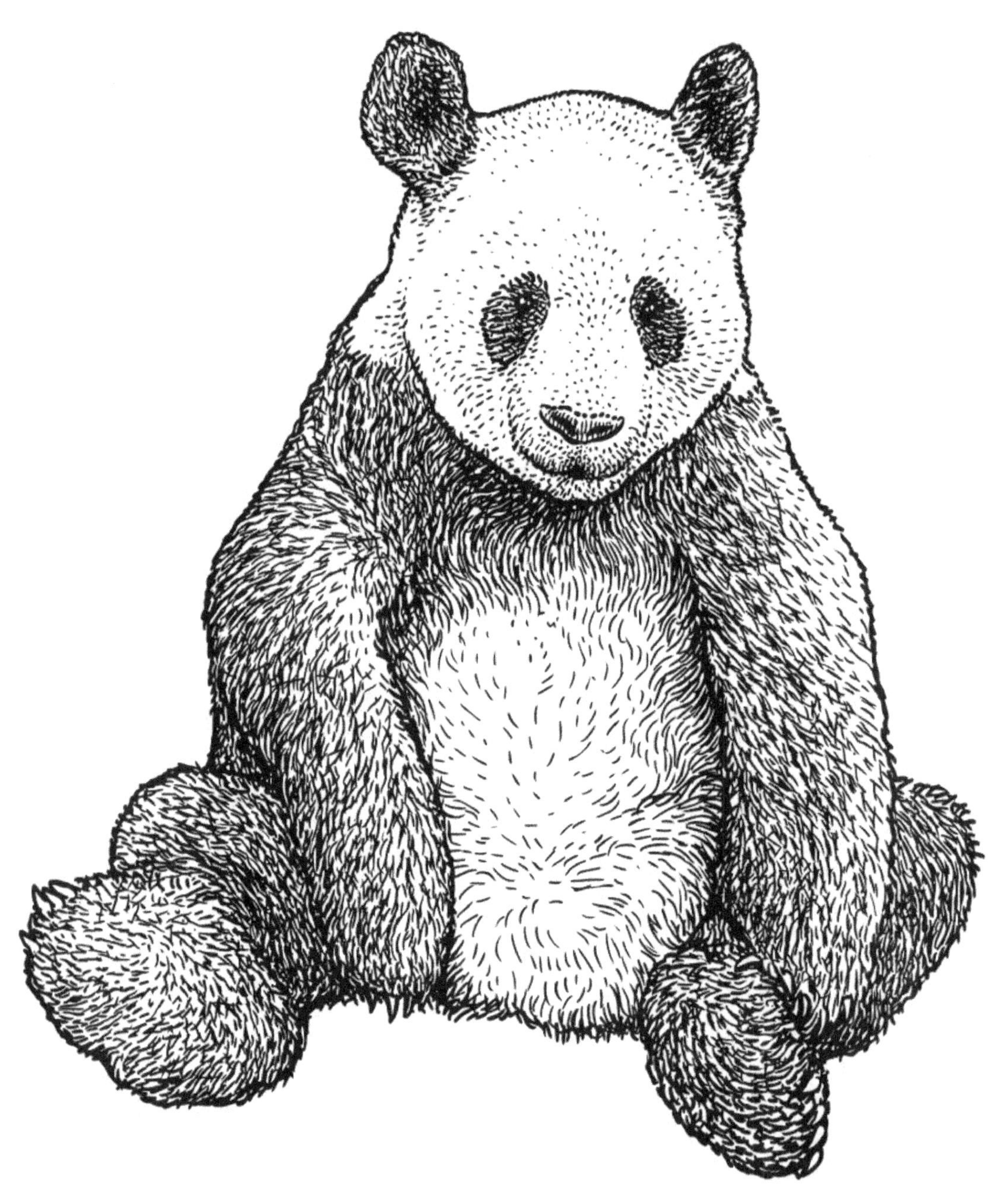

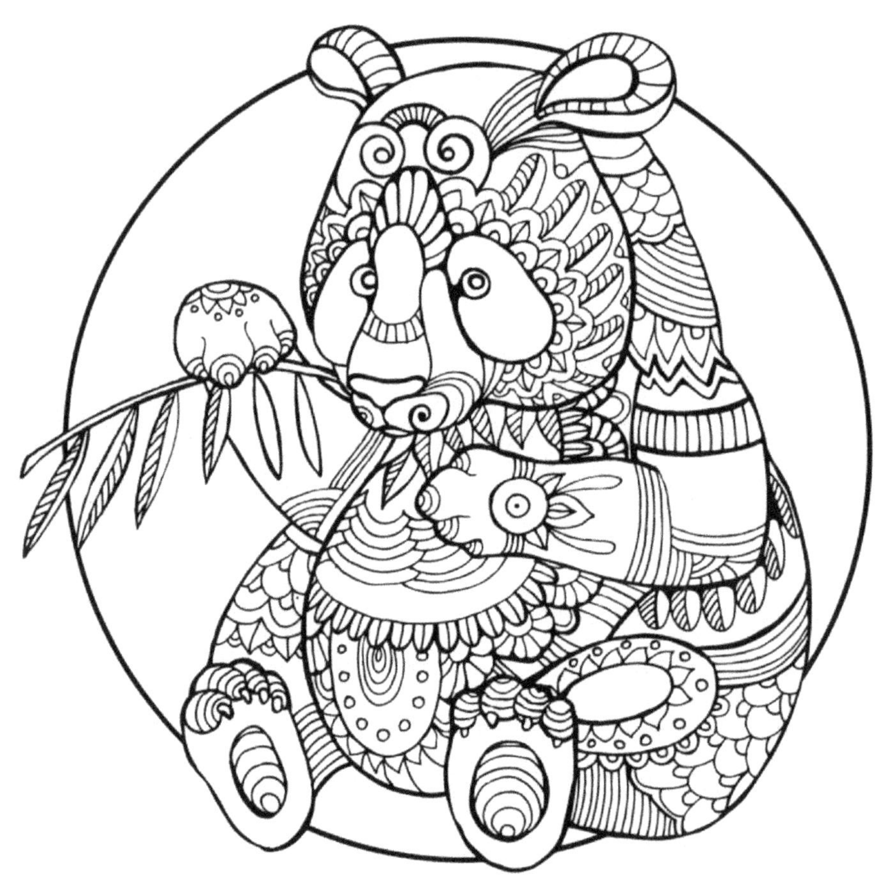

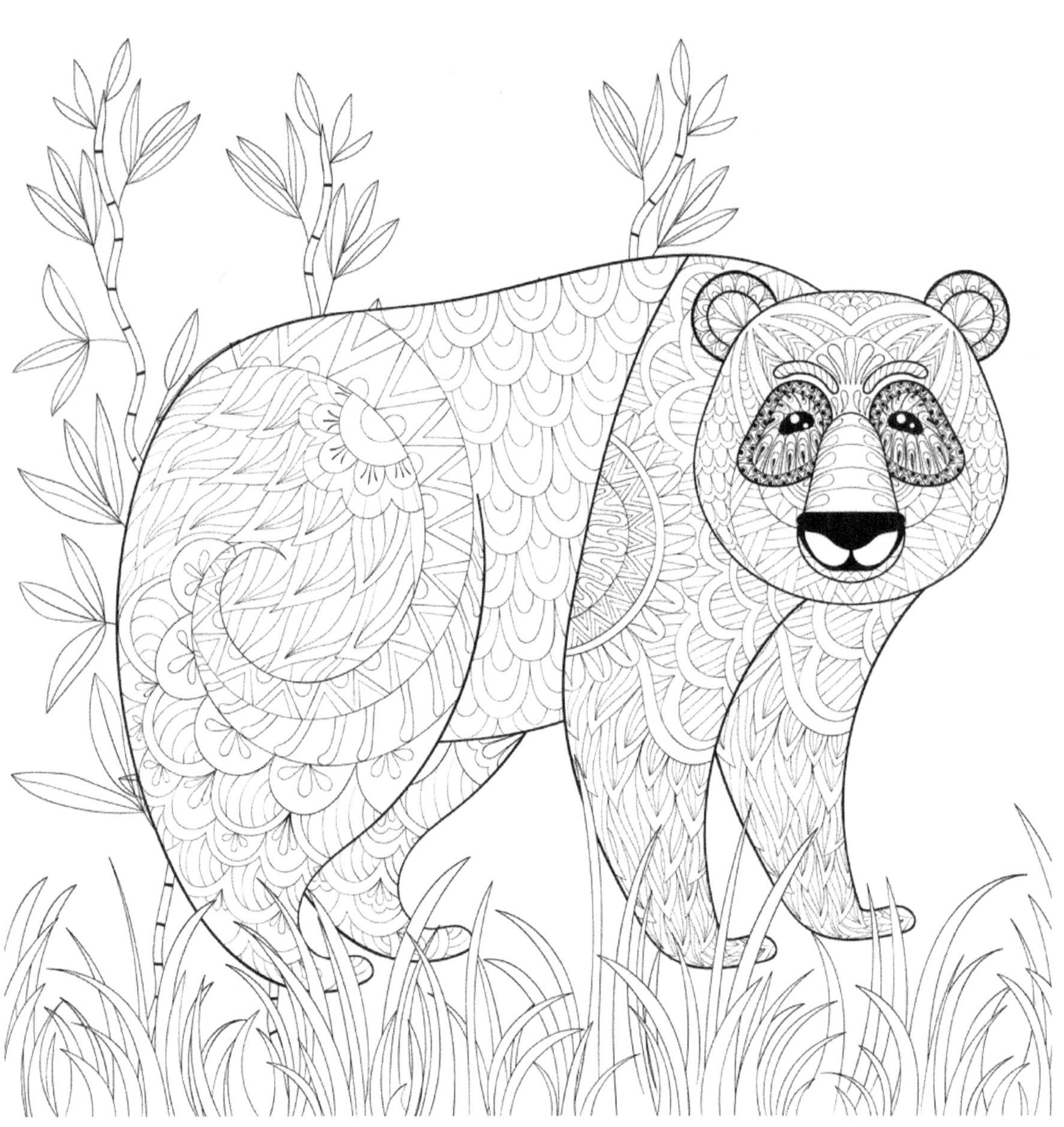

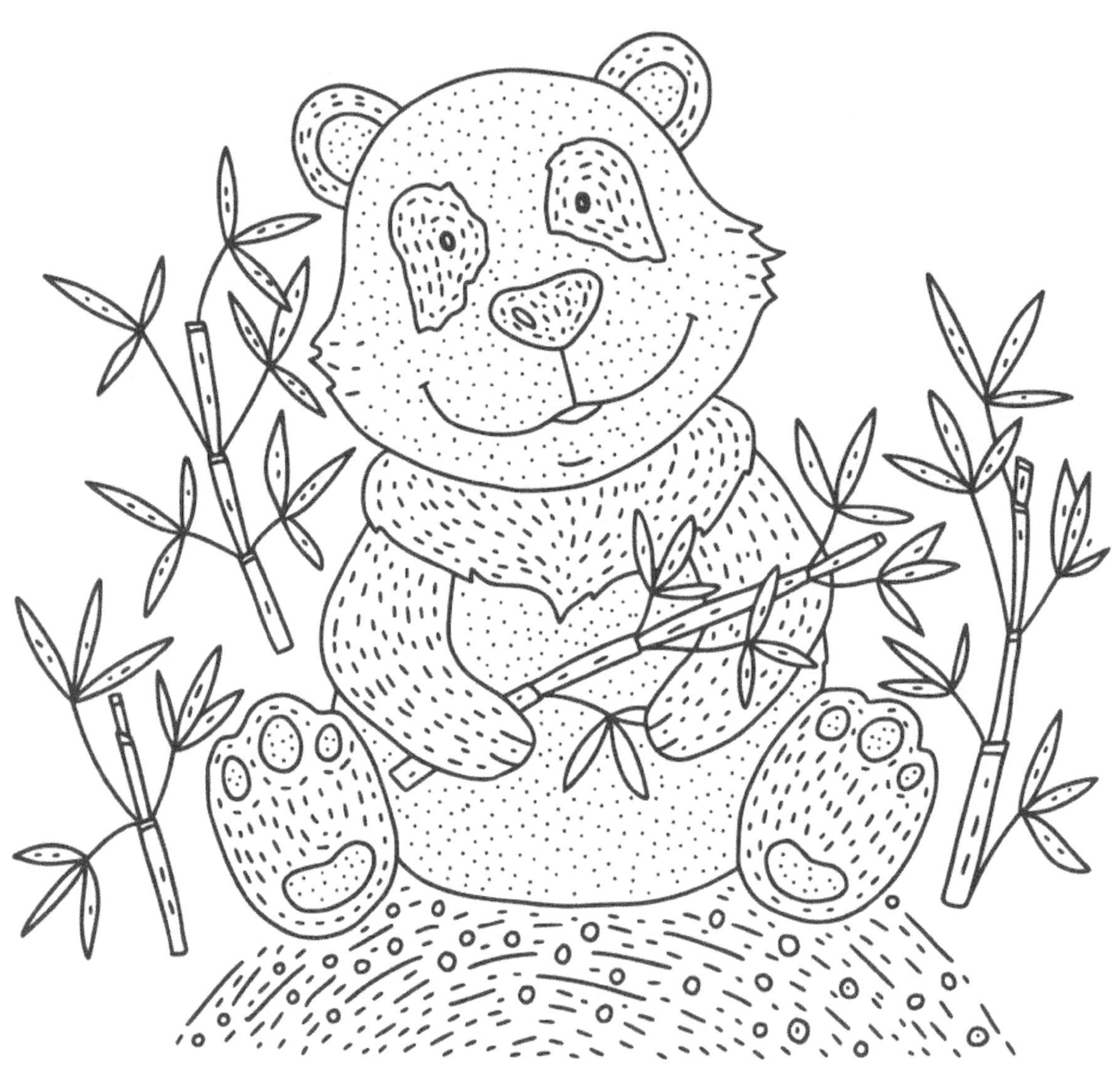

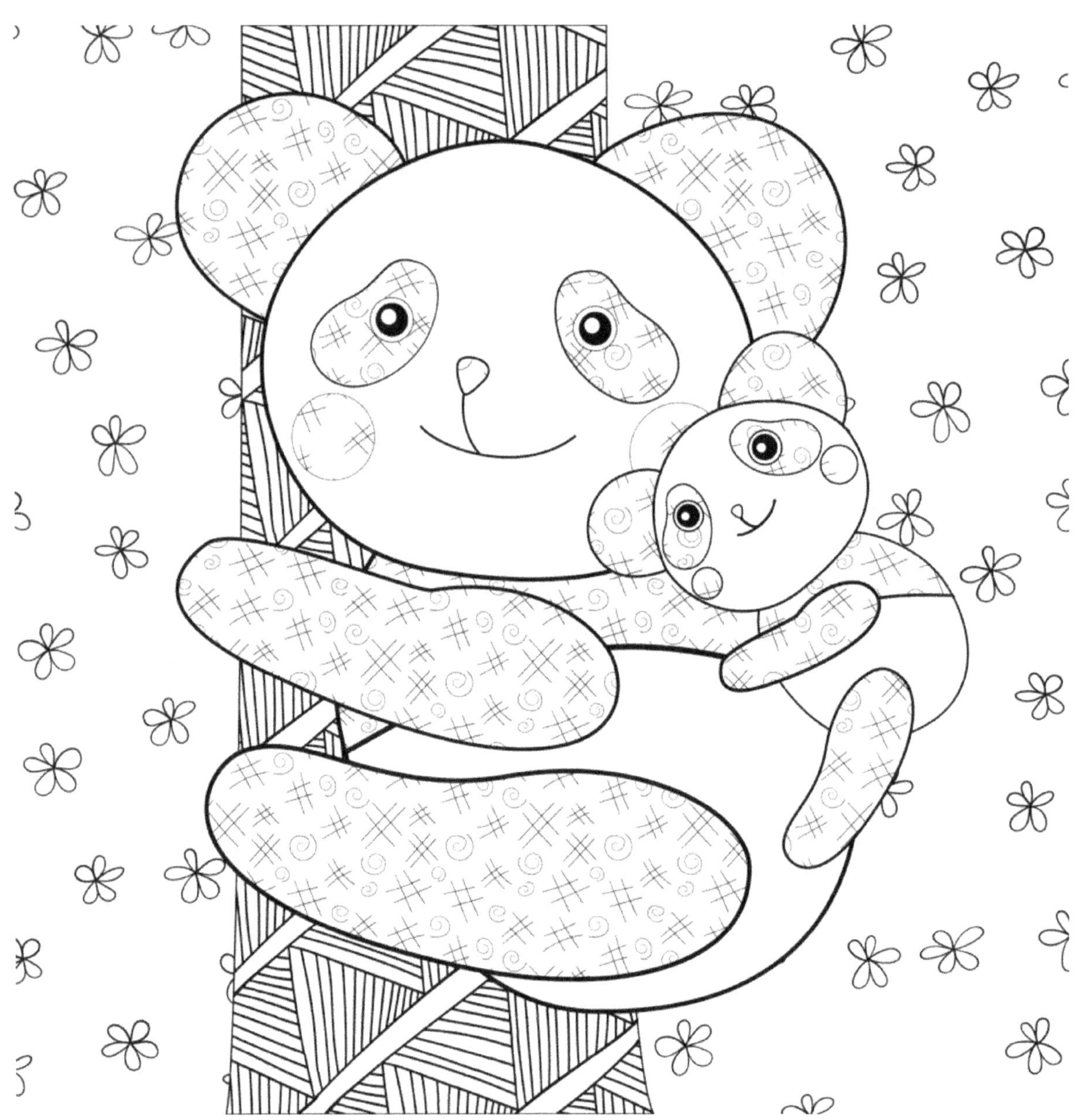

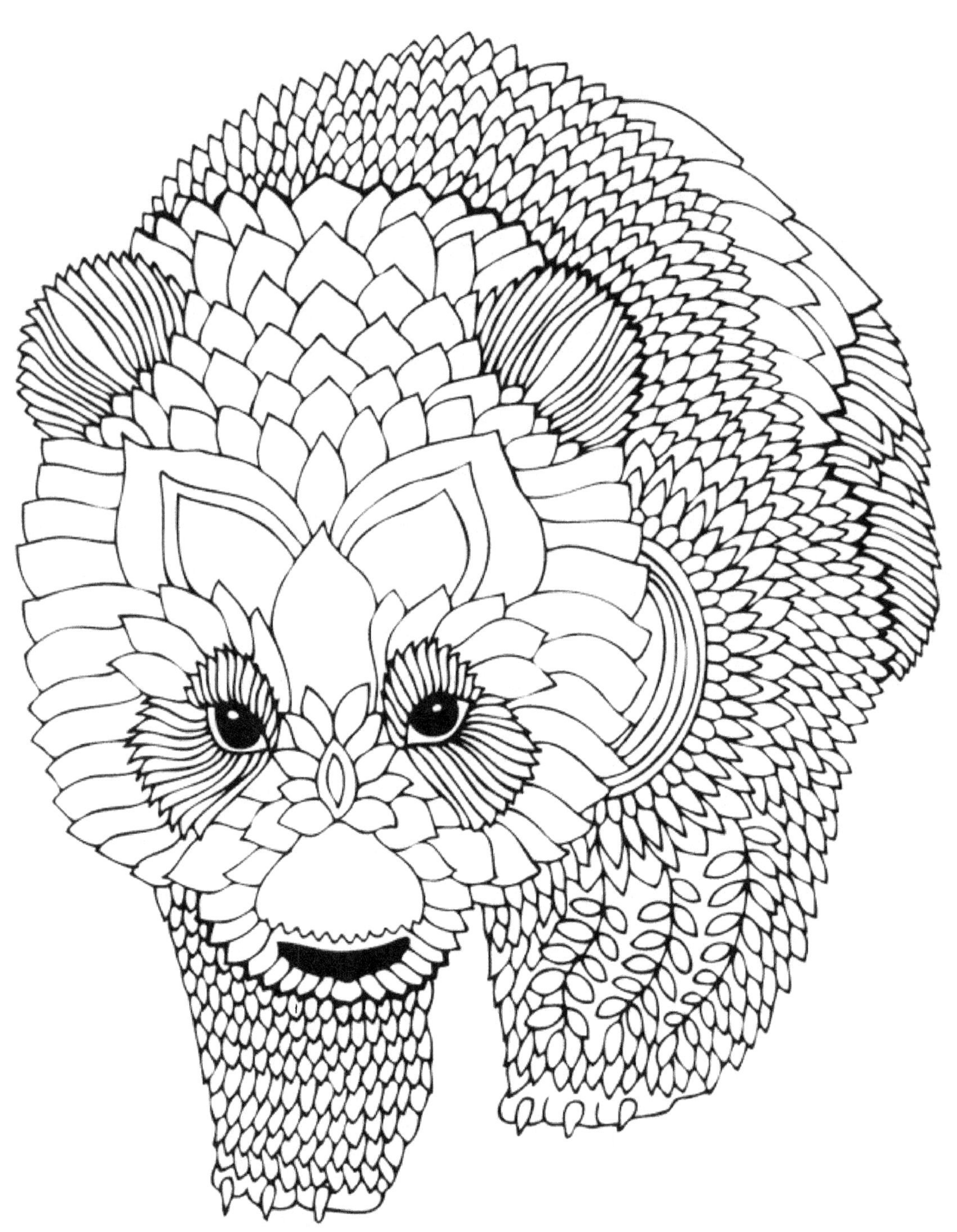

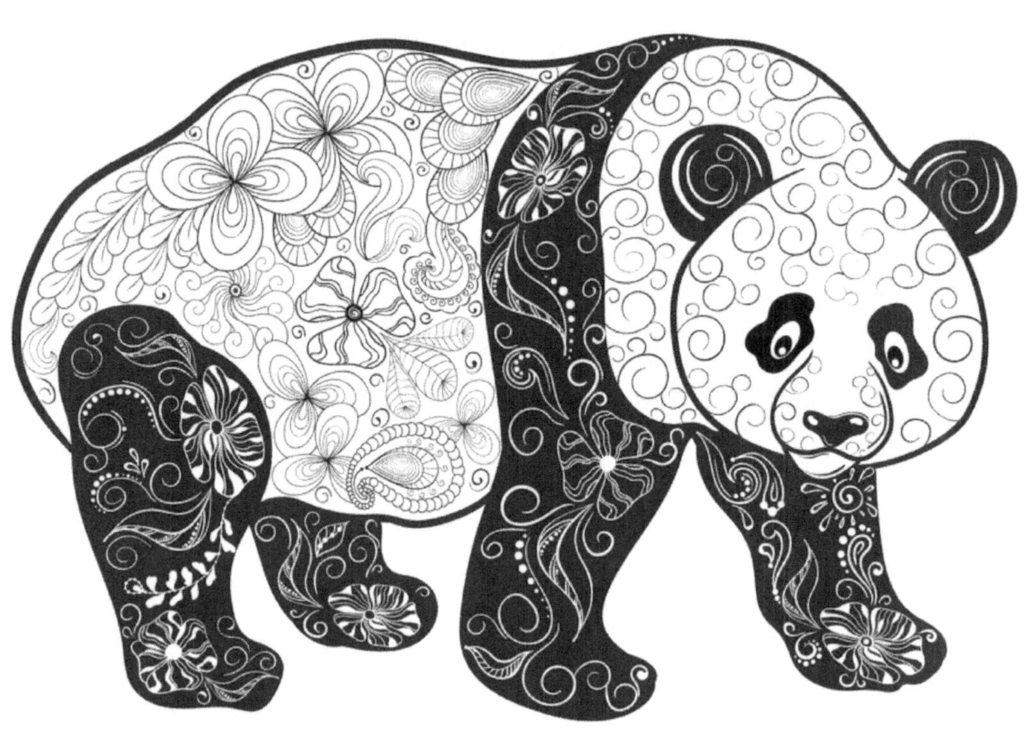

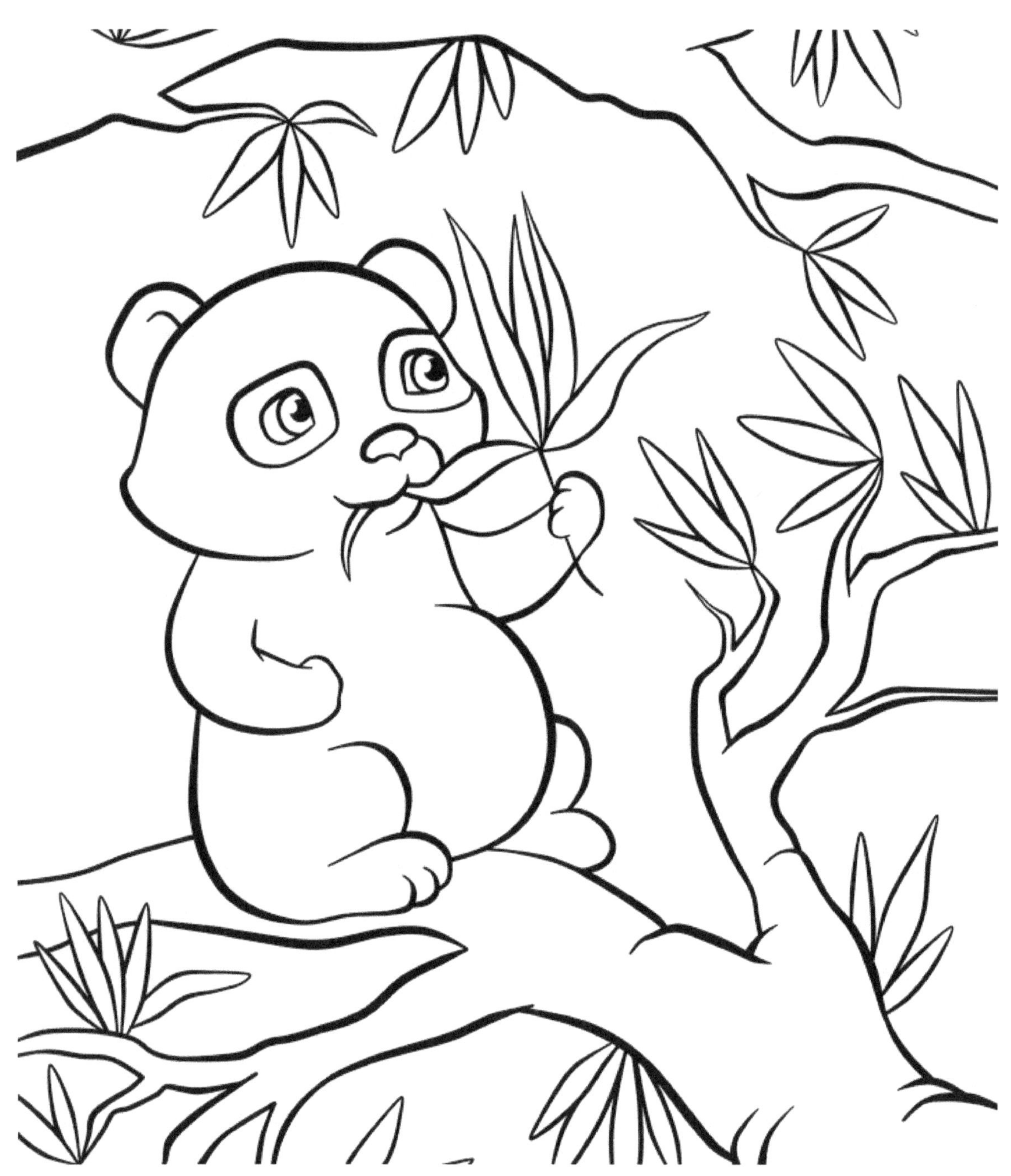

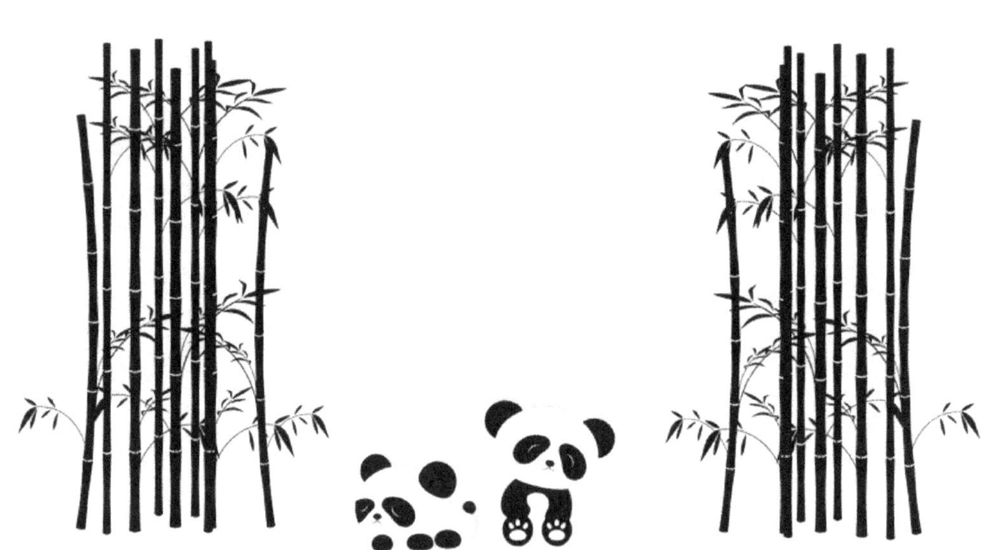

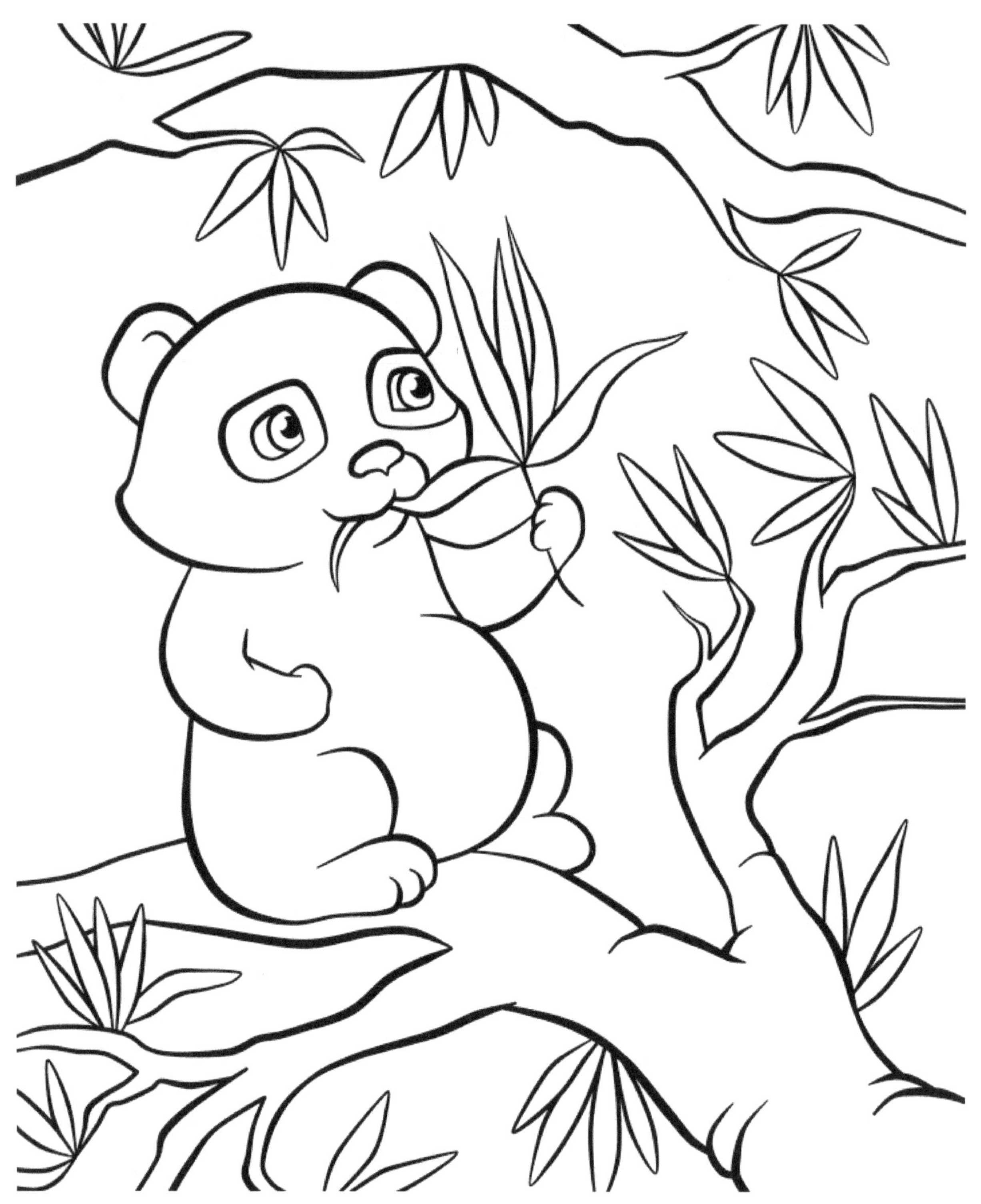

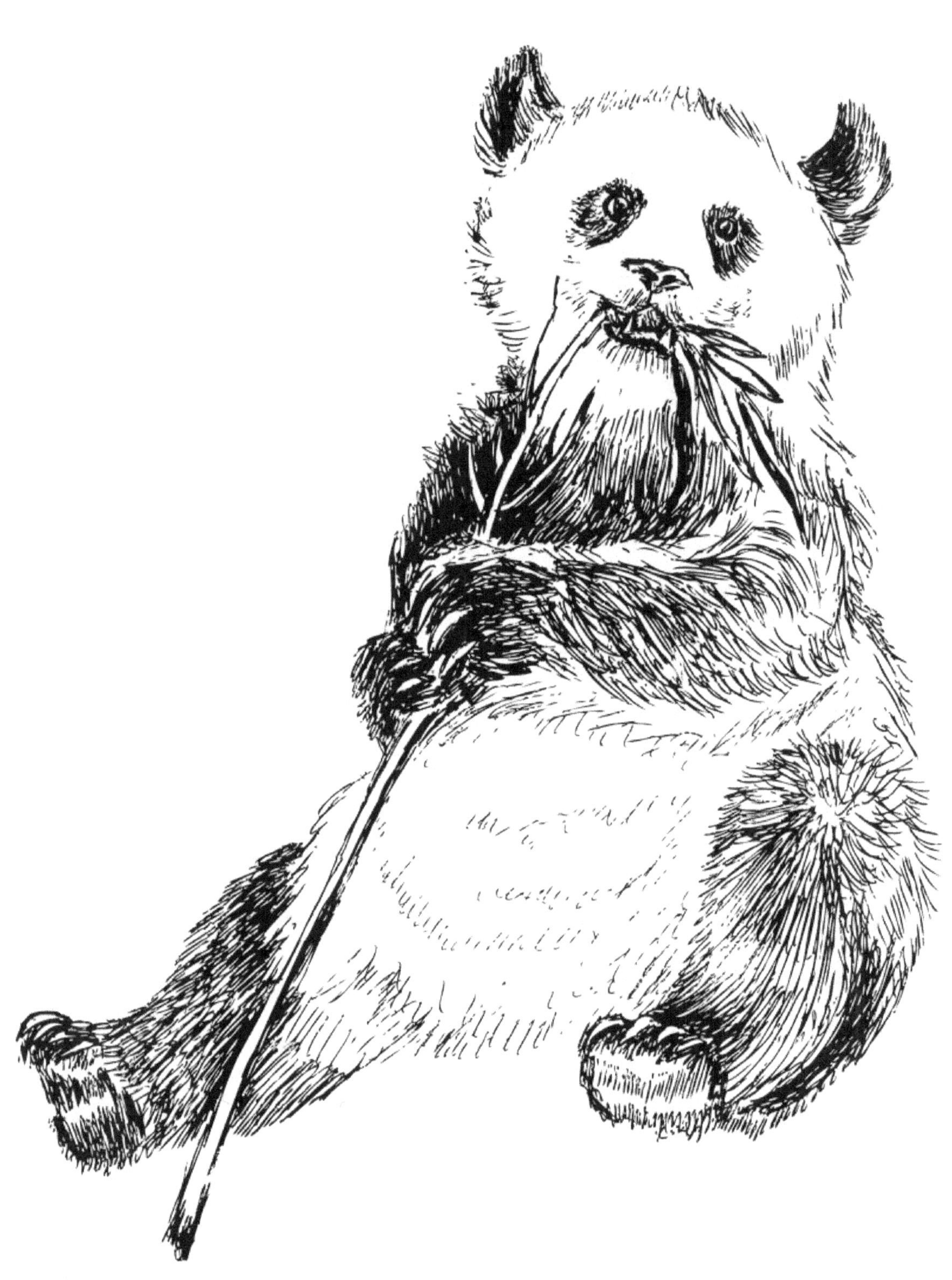

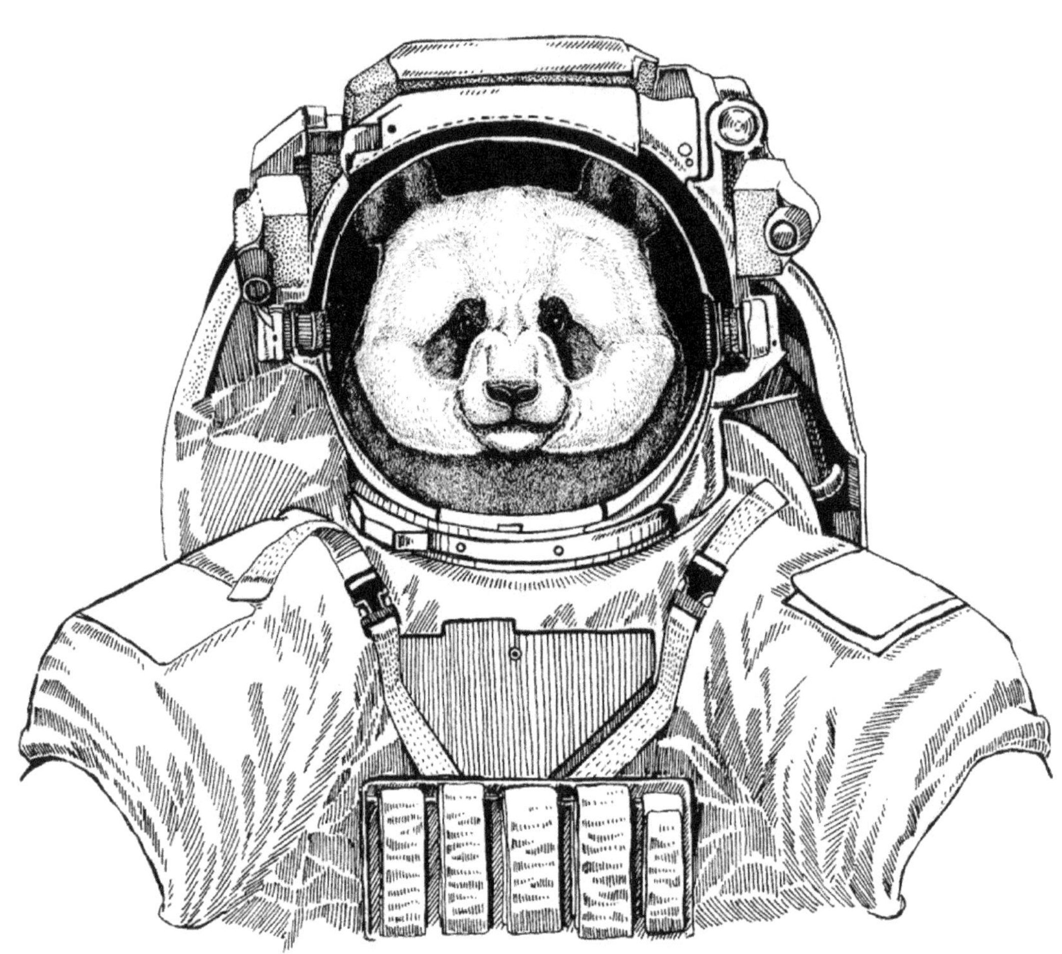

I NEED MORE SPACE

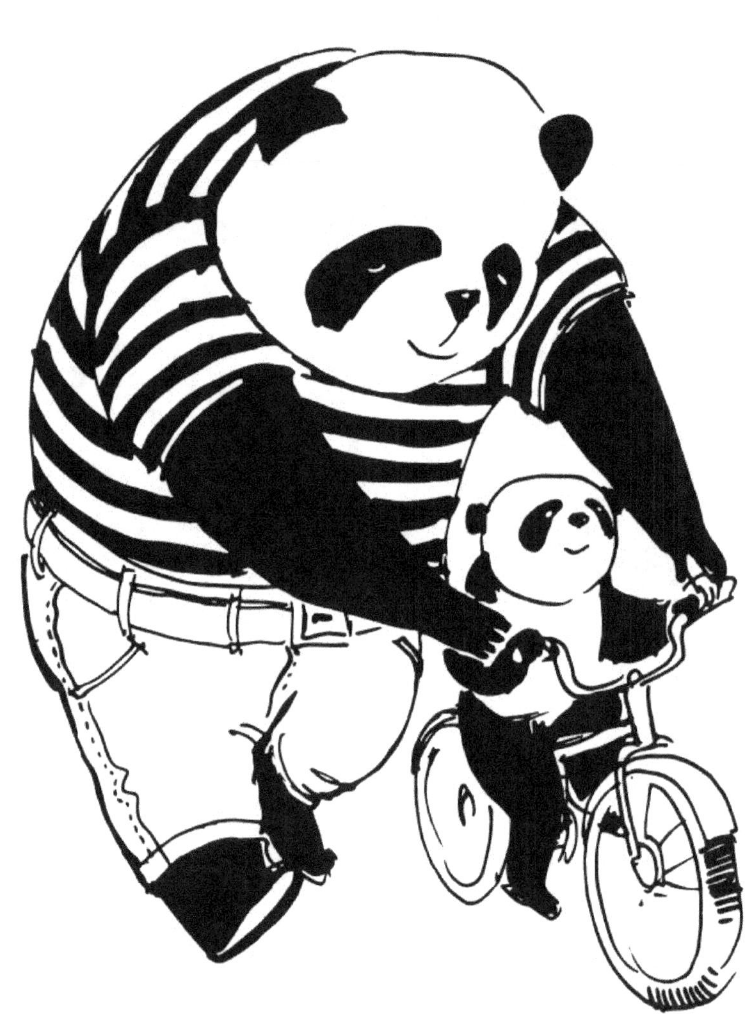

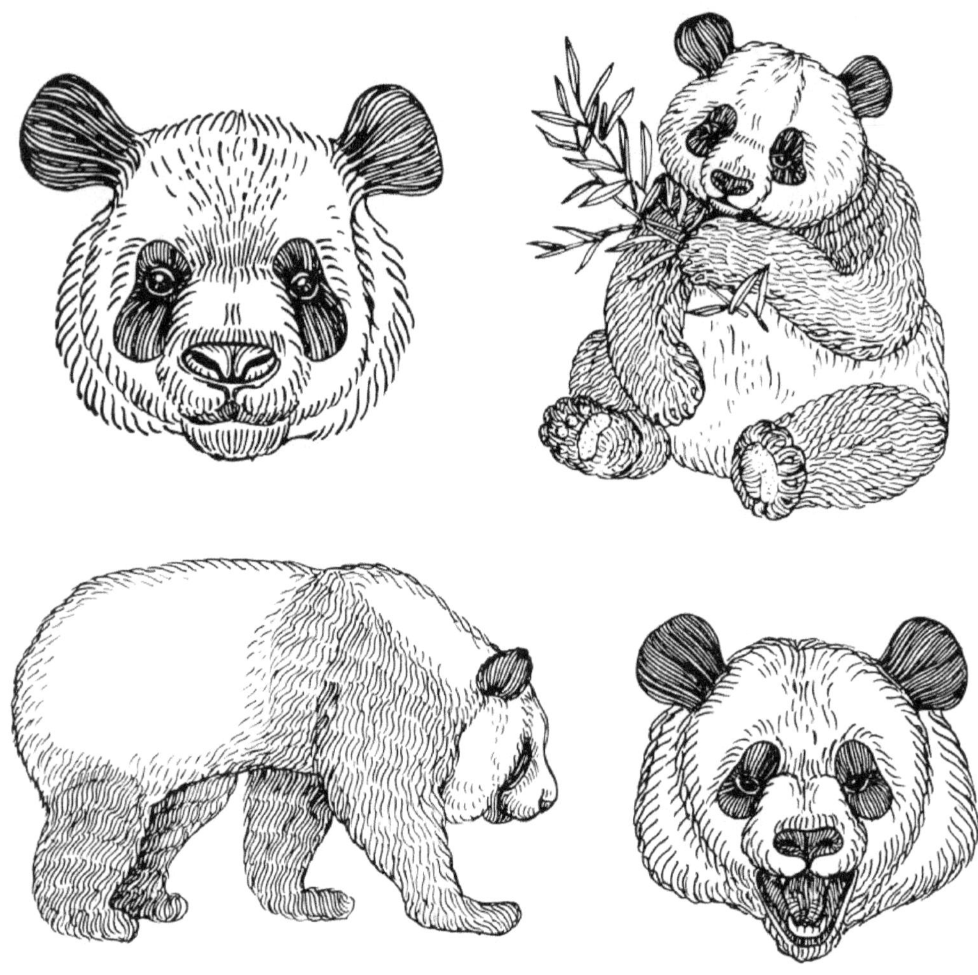

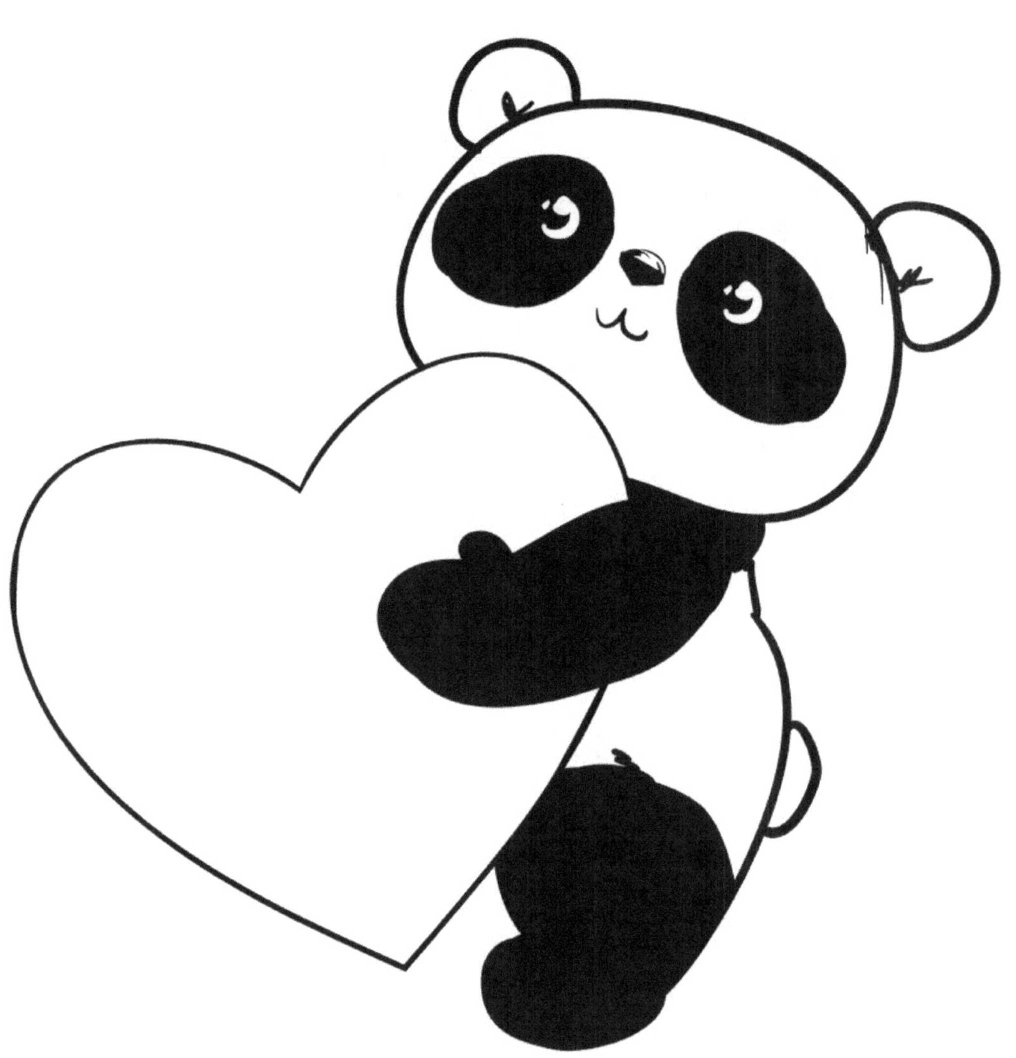

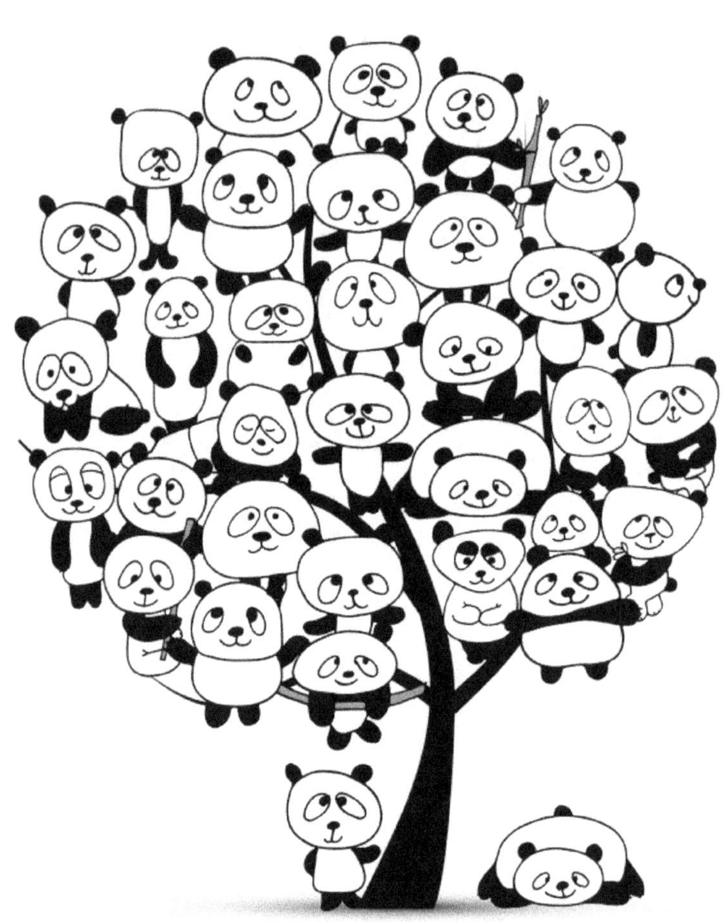

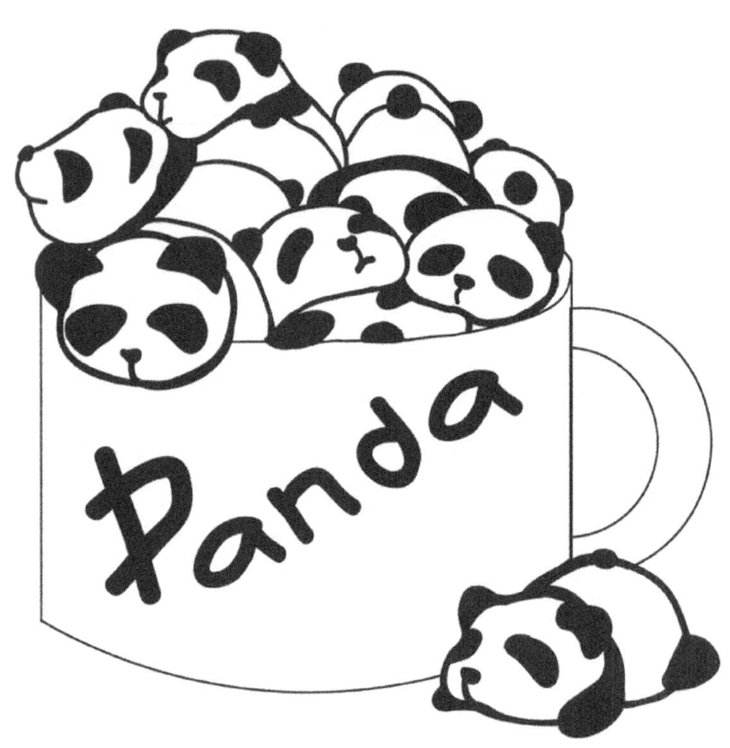

Panda

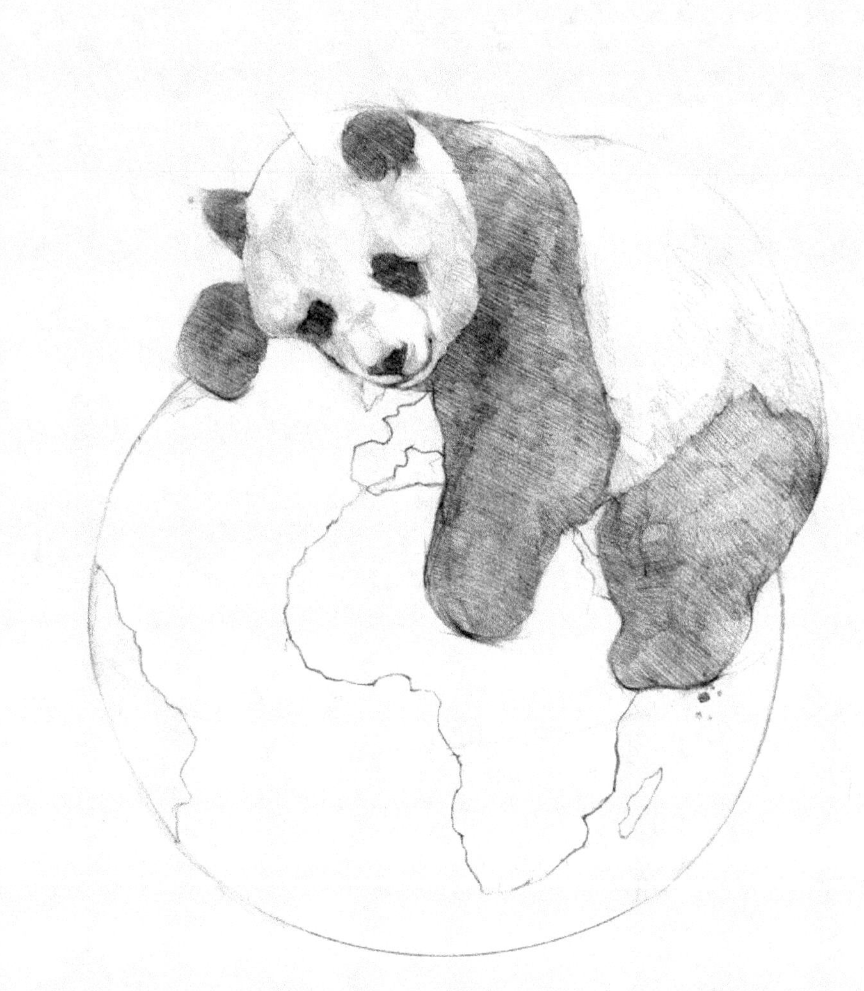

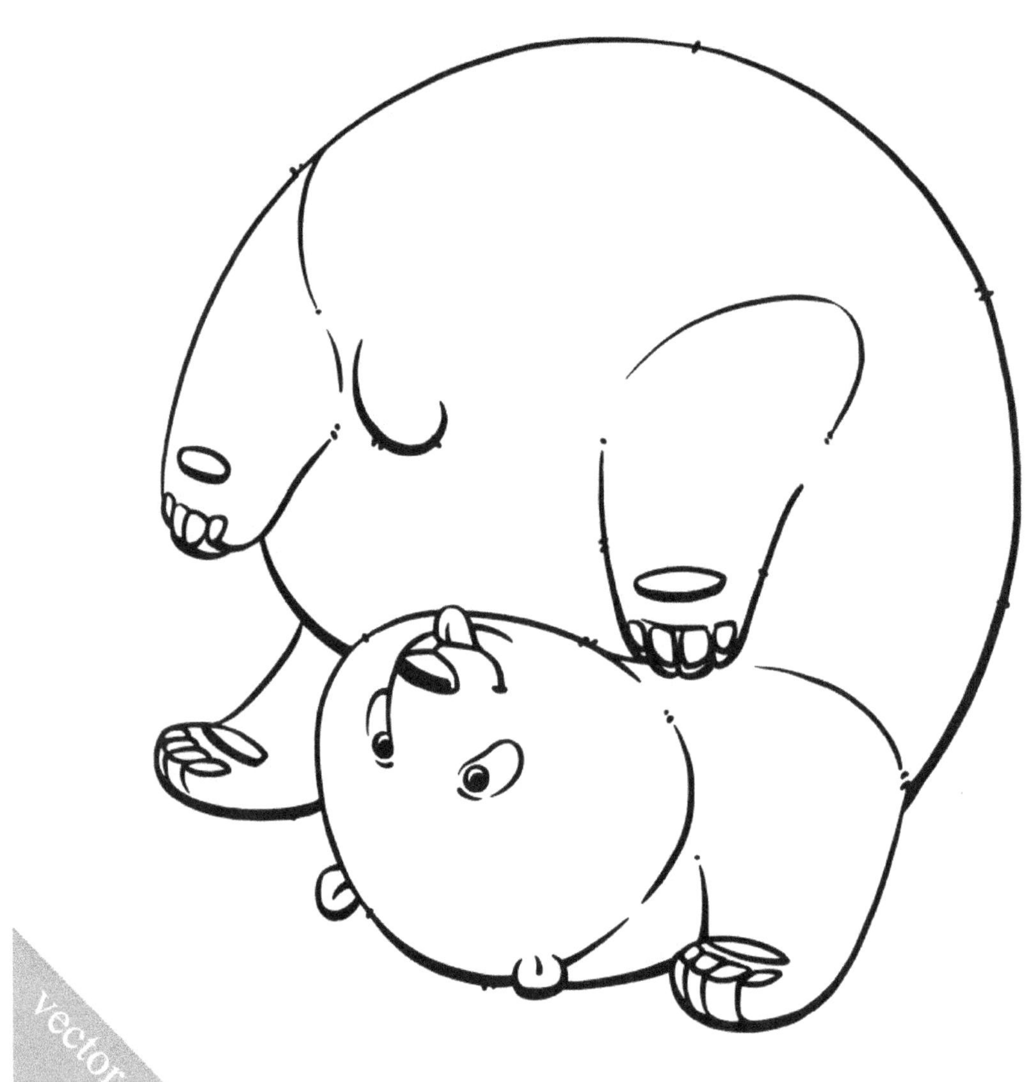

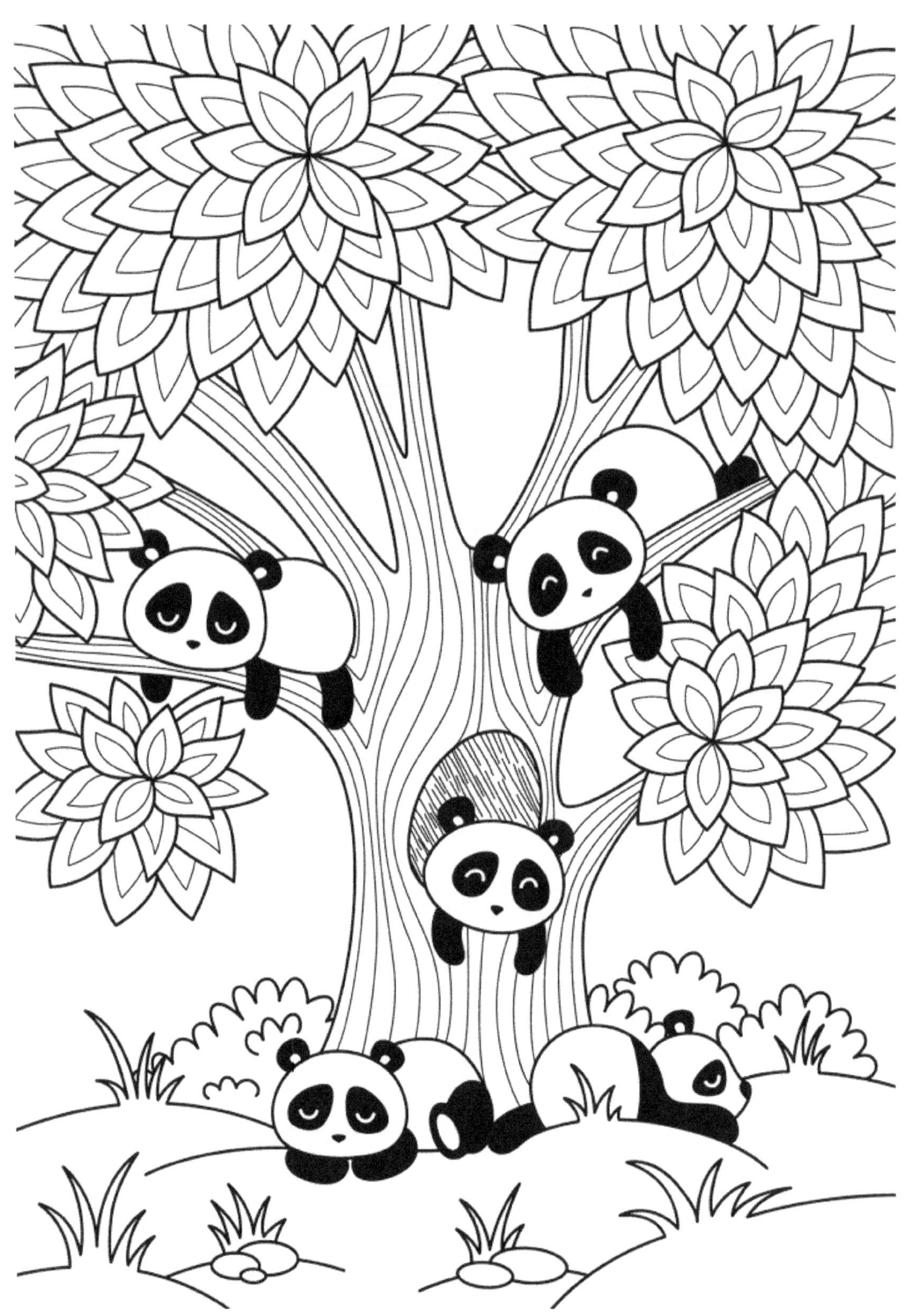

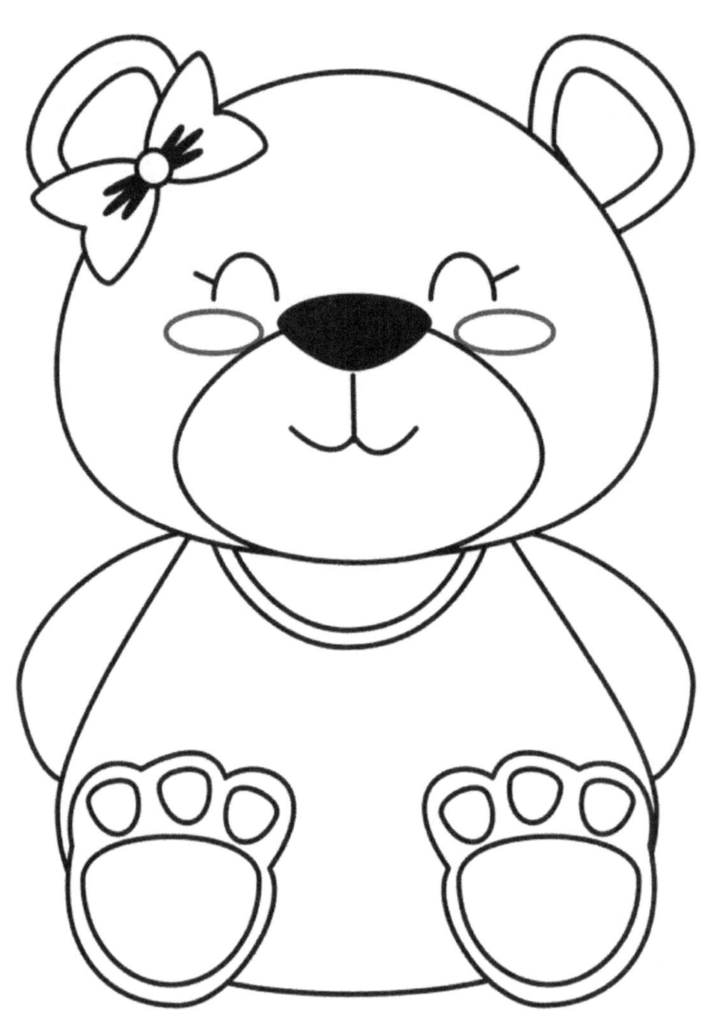

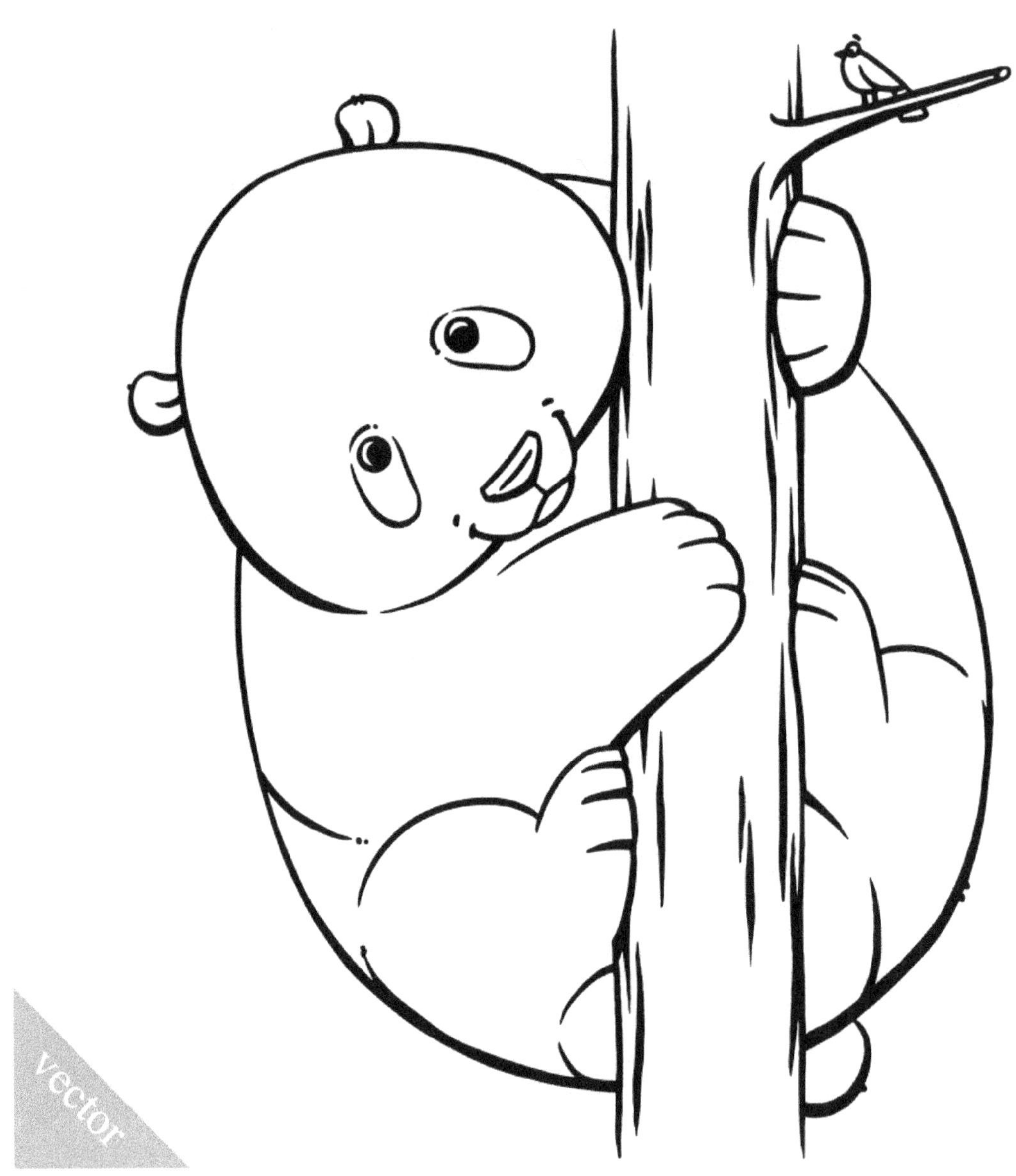

vector

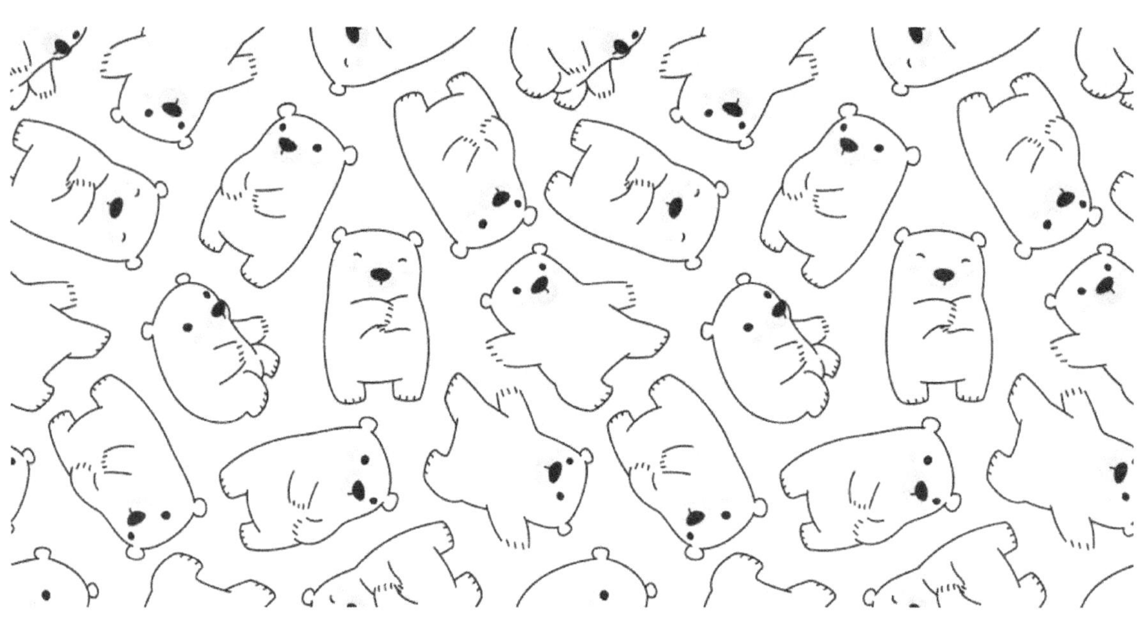

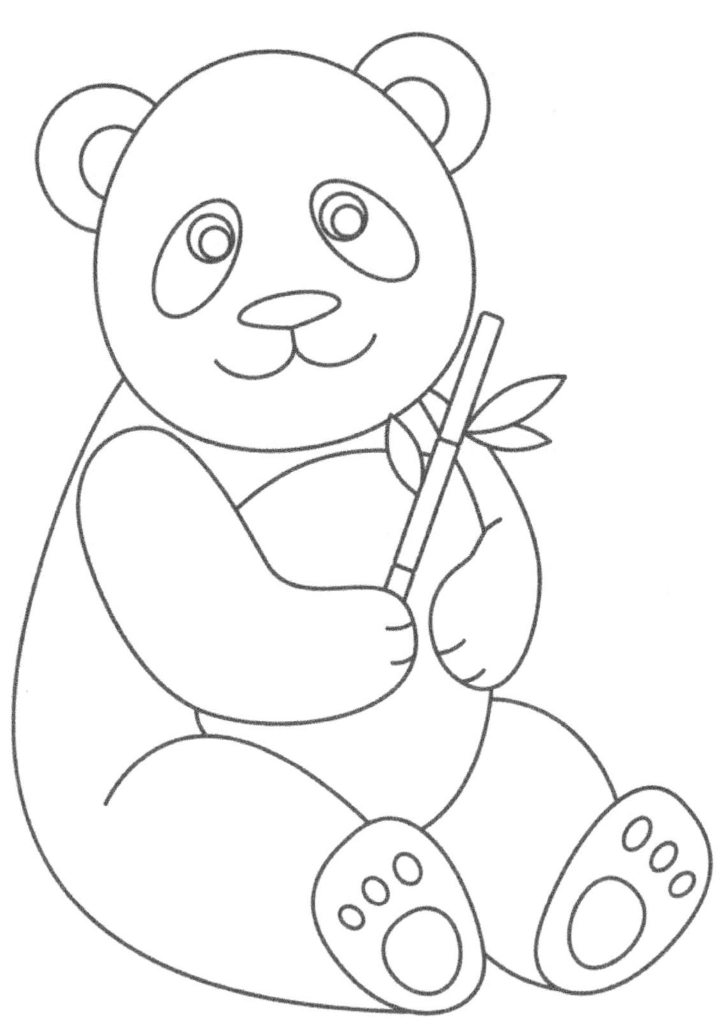

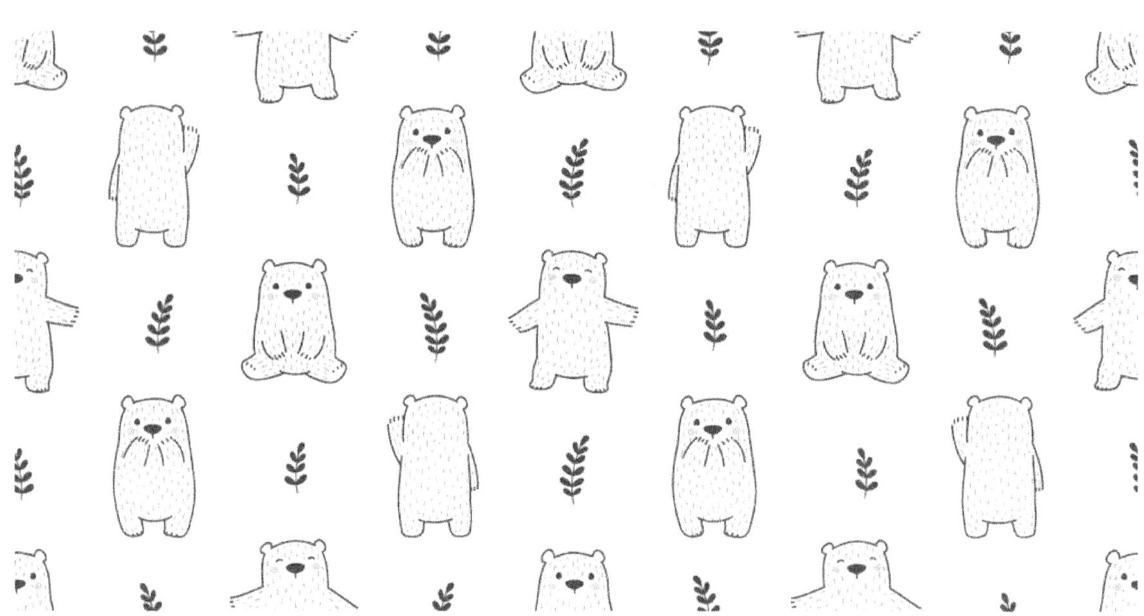

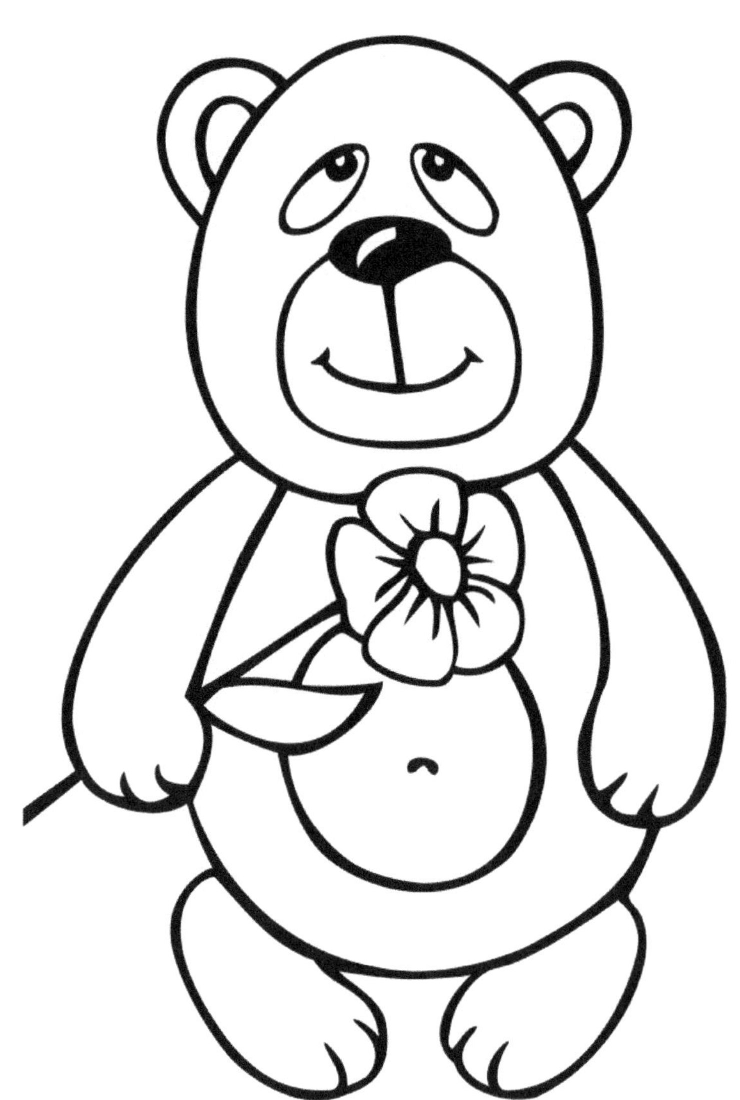

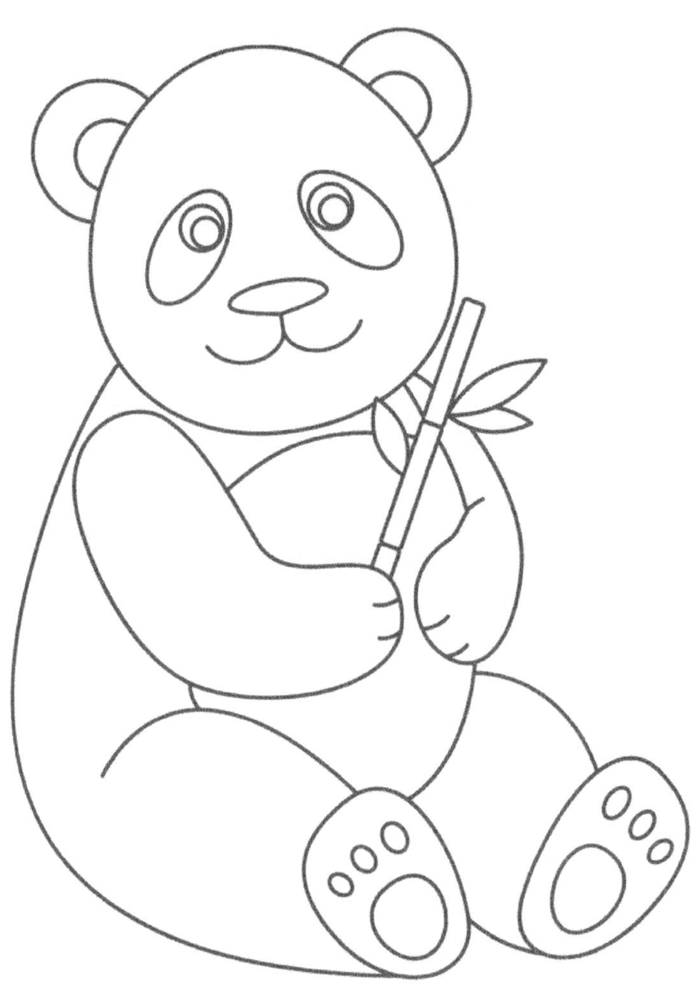

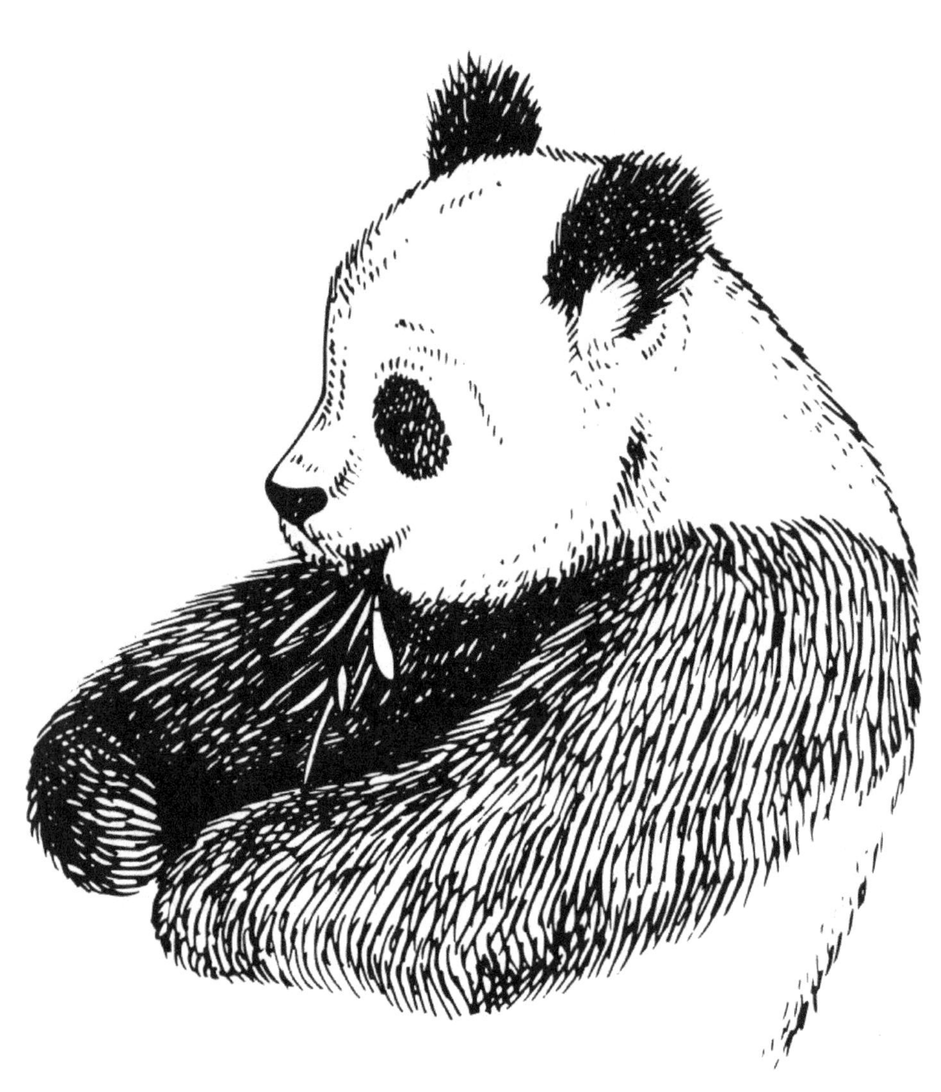

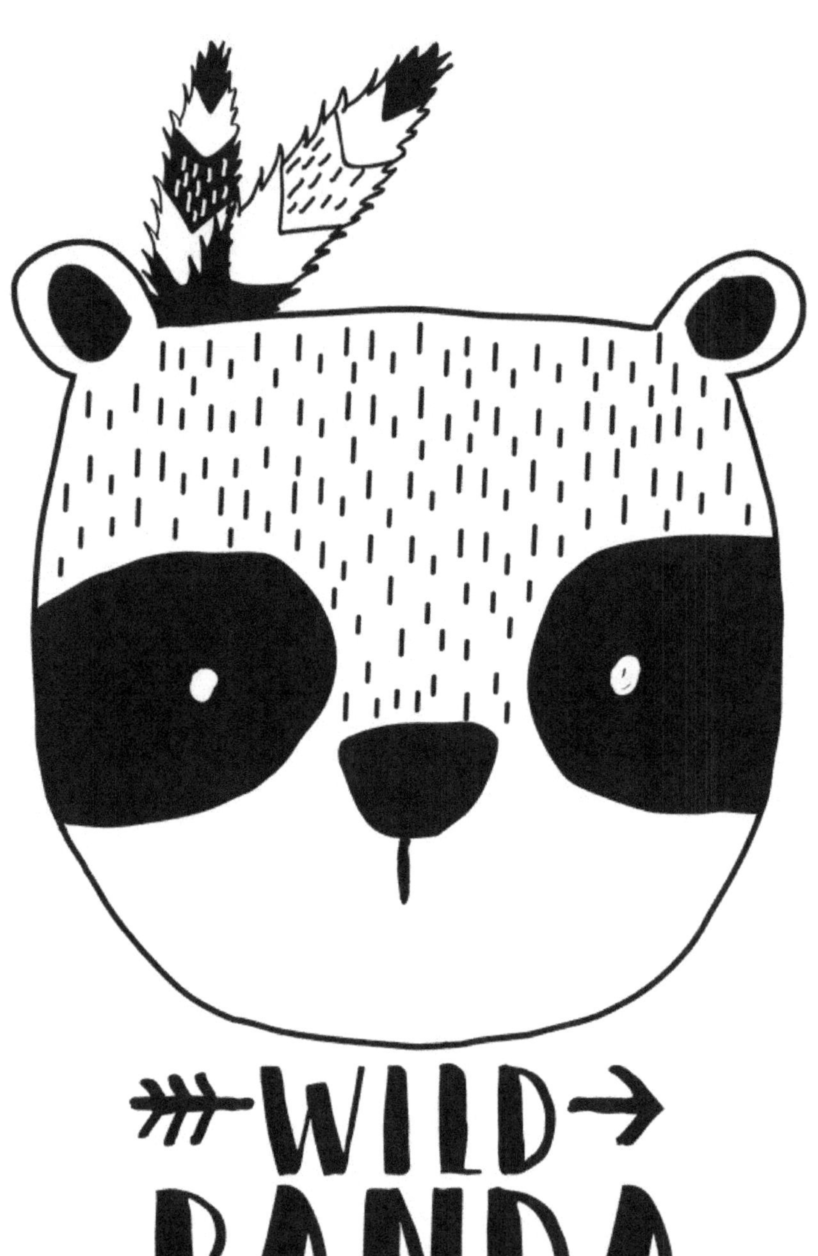

WILD
PANDA

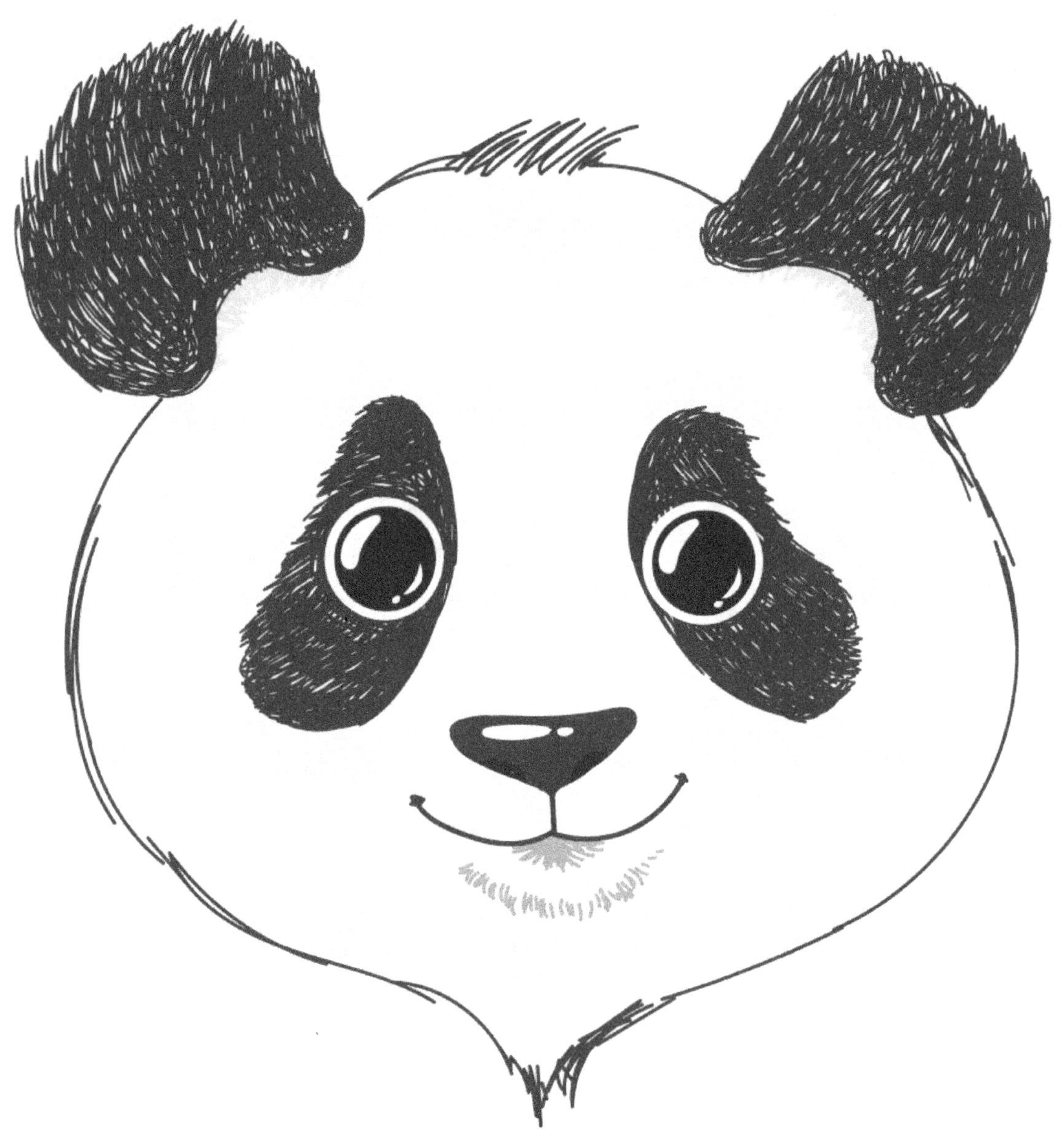